Original title:
Wisps of Wonder

Copyright © 2024 Creative Arts Management OÜ
All rights reserved.

Author: Juliette Kensington
ISBN HARDBACK: 978-9916-90-538-8
ISBN PAPERBACK: 978-9916-90-539-5

Veils of Mystery

In shadows deep, secrets dwell,
Whispers of time, a hidden spell.
Each glance reveals what hearts conceal,
A dance of dreams, a silent wheel.

Beneath the moon's soft, watchful gaze,
Entranced we wander through the haze.
Mystic paths where visions gleam,
Cloaked in silence, lost in dream.

Fragments of Bliss

A gentle breeze, a soft embrace,
Moments cherished, time can't erase.
Laughter dances on the air,
In every heart, love waits somewhere.

Petals falling, colors bright,
Fleeting joys in morning light.
Fragments held in memories sweet,
Life's simple joys, a rare retreat.

Celestial Whispers

Stars awaken in the night,
Softly glowing, pure delight.
Cosmic tales in silence spun,
Universes, two as one.

Galaxies whisper from afar,
Dreaming of who we truly are.
In the stillness, souls take flight,
Boundless love in cosmic light.

Dances of the Lighthearted

Laughter twirls on sunshine's beam,
Life unfolds like a joyous dream.
Steps of joy on grassy knolls,
Echoes of free and carefree souls.

Clouds drift by in skies of blue,
Days of wonder, fresh and new.
With every step, the heart takes flight,
In the dance of the lighthearted night.

Enigmatic Reflections

In shadows deep, we wander lost,
Questions linger, at what cost?
Mirrors whisper secrets loud,
In silent rooms, beneath the shroud.

Thoughts like ripples in a pond,
Searching for what lies beyond.
Answers dance just out of sight,
Fleeting forms in soft twilight.

Cascades of Color

Painted skies at break of dawn,
Nature's brush, a vibrant song.
Rivers flow in hues of gold,
Stories of the world untold.

Petals fall like whispered dreams,
In gardens bright, where sunlight beams.
Every shade a tale to tell,
In this canvas where we dwell.

The Glow of the Ordinary

Simple moments, pure and clear,
A smile shared, a heart sincere.
In cups of tea and soft goodbyes,
Life unfolds in quiet sighs.

Starlit nights and morning dew,
Little things that speak so true.
Finding joy in mundane days,
Life's hidden gems in countless ways.

Effervescent Echoes

Laughter bubbles, rising high,
In the air, where spirits fly.
Memories dance, a lively tune,
Underneath a silver moon.

Whispers of the past remain,
In every joy, in every pain.
Echoes linger, soft and sweet,
In our hearts, where loved ones meet.

Twinkles in Twilight

Stars above begin to gleam,
In the hush of day's retreat.
Whispers float on gentle streams,
Where sun and moon softly meet.

Colors fade to dusky gray,
As night drapes its velvet cloak.
Dreams and wishes start to play,
In the stillness, voices spoke.

Crickets sing their evening song,
Nature sways in twilight's dance.
Each bright twinkle feels so strong,
Guiding hearts in moonlit trance.

Shadows of the Heart

In the corner, secrets sigh,
Echoed tales of love's refrain.
Silent whispers pass on by,
Each a dream, a joy, or pain.

Lost in moments, time can bend,
Fleeting glances, bittersweet.
Every heart must learn to mend,
Crafting stories, bittersweet.

Flickers of light chase the dusk,
In the shadows, truths unfold.
Through the darkness, find the trust,
In the warmth of hands to hold.

Symphony of the Subtle

Notes of silence start to weave,
Softly playing on the air.
Every breath feels like a leaf,
Drifting gently without care.

Melodies of softest hues,
Whispers brush against the soul.
In this dance, we cannot lose,
As the world begins to roll.

Harmony in gentle dreams,
Echoing through every heart.
In the quiet, love redeems,
Binding souls that will not part.

Mysterious Caresses

Fingers trace a secret line,
Mapping constellations bright.
In the dark, the stars align,
Filling shadows with their light.

Touch of night, a velvet kiss,
Softly wraps the world in grace.
In each whisper, purest bliss,
Hearts entwined in slow embrace.

Through the night's enchanting song,
Every beat a mystery.
In the silence, we belong,
Dancing in the history.

Chasing Enigmas

In shadows deep, we wander slow,
Whispers of truth begin to glow.
Questions linger, mysteries play,
Chasing enigmas, night and day.

Footsteps echo on silent ground,
In the unknown, lost and found.
Stars above, secrets unfold,
Timeless tales waiting to be told.

Through fog and light, illusions blend,
Puzzles woven, twists that bend.
With every clue, our hearts take flight,
Chasing enigmas through the night.

Each riddle brings a spark of hope,
In the labyrinth, we learn to cope.
With every turn, the world expands,
Chasing enigmas, hand in hands.

Dances of the Enchanted

In moonlit glades where shadows sway,
Dances of the enchanted play.
Fae and whispers blend with night,
Twinkling stars, a wondrous sight.

Echoes of laughter fill the air,
Magic weaves through flowing hair.
With every step, the earth will sing,
In this realm where fairies wing.

Petals twirl in a gentle breeze,
Joined by song, among the trees.
Hearts enraptured, spirits soar,
Dances of magic evermore.

Through the shadows, the joy will bloom,
Casting light amidst the gloom.
Under the stars, together we prance,
Lost forever in the enchanted dance.

Glances at the Ethereal

Glimmers of light on dusky waves,
Glances at the ethereal, dreams it saves.
In fleeting moments, we catch a sight,
Of worlds beyond, both strange and bright.

Veils of twilight, softly drawn,
In the silence, the magic's born.
Hearts aglow with celestial fire,
Reaching out for something higher.

Each glance a portal, a fleeting key,
Unlocking wonders, wild and free.
Through the haze, visions call,
In the ethereal, we rise, we fall.

With open hearts, we dare to see,
The tapestry woven, you and me.
In kaleidoscopes of love and light,
Glances at the ethereal, pure delight.

Secrets in the Air

Whispers linger, secrets unfurl,
Floating softly in this world.
In the breeze, tales gently sway,
Secrets in the air, come what may.

Echoing dreams, stories untold,
In every sigh, a truth unfolds.
With every breath, the earth will sigh,
Secrets in the air, bittersweet cry.

At twilight's edge, shadows encroach,
Silent murmurs, thoughts we broach.
Through the stillness, we clearly hear,
Secrets in the air, ever near.

So listen close, let your heart share,
The silent truths found everywhere.
In every moment, love and care,
Breathe in deeply, secrets in the air.

Lanterns of Hope

In the dark where shadows play,
Softly glows a distant ray.
Whispers of a brighter dawn,
Guiding hearts where love is drawn.

Flickering, the lights will sway,
Promising a brand new day.
Through the night, we find our way,
Hope anew, we'll never stray.

Murmurs of Discovery

Listen close to the gentle breeze,
Secrets carried through the trees.
Every rustle tells a tale,
Of whispers soft like ocean's veil.

Footsteps dance on ancient ground,
In the silence, truths are found.
Curiosity leads the heart,
In the search, we play our part.

Illusions in the Mist

Veils of gray caress the land,
Shapes emerge, like dreams unplanned.
Figures fade as quickly seen,
In the fog, what lies between?

A world where nothing's as it seems,
Swaying softly, held in dreams.
Reality drifts, a shadow's kiss,
Embrace the magic in the abyss.

Petals of Mystery

Softly falling, whispers bright,
Petals drift in the soft twilight.
Ochre, crimson, shades divine,
In their quiet dance, they shine.

Every blossom, a tale untold,
Cradled gently, petals fold.
As they land, a secret shared,
In their beauty, we have dared.

Intrigues of the Heart

In shadows deep, secrets play,
Tender tales in quiet sway.
Whispers float on dreamy nights,
Starlit paths reveal their lights.

Yearning glances, hearts collide,
Unspoken truths we dare not hide.
Threads of fate weaves love's design,
In each heartbeat, souls entwine.

Wandering Whispers

Underneath the ancient trees,
Softly murmurs drift with ease.
Secrets shared in rustling leaves,
Nature's voice, the heart believes.

Echoes linger, soft and sweet,
Guiding footsteps where dreams meet.
Through the dusk, a tale unfolds,
In the silence, love retolds.

Traces on the Wind

Gentle breezes carry light,
Fleeting images in flight.
Memories whispered, lost yet found,
In each gust, their songs resound.

Footprints on the sands of time,
Soft reminders, rhythms rhyme.
As the seasons turn and sway,
Love's imprint forever stays.

Glowing Echoes

In twilight hues, the world gleams,
Radiant whispers cradle dreams.
Shadows dance with golden light,
Embers glow in the heart's sight.

Through the dark, the spirits sing,
Hope ignites with each new spring.
In the silence, love's refrain,
Glowing echoes shall remain.

Dreams upon the Breeze

Whispers in the night skies,
Carried on winds so free,
Thoughts of hope arise,
In every swaying tree.

Pictures painted bright,
In the moon's soft glow,
Chasing fading light,
To where the dreamers go.

Stories made of stars,
Traveling far and wide,
Breaking down the bars,
Of drifting worlds inside.

With every breath we take,
We dance along the tide,
In dreams, we shall awake,
With nothing left to hide.

Cascades of the Unexplained

Mysteries descend,
From cliffs so high and steep,
Whispers never end,
In shadows where we leap.

Ripples in the stream,
Hide stories yet untold,
Potions of a dream,
In twilight's arms, we hold.

Leaves swirl in the air,
Cascading thoughts that flow,
Into unknown layers,
Where secrets softly grow.

The heart begins to race,
As wonders intertwine,
In this sacred space,
The unknown's pure design.

Ephemeral Dreams

Fleeting like the dawn,
Bright flashes in the night,
A canvas gently drawn,
In shadows painted light.

Petals on the stream,
Drifting in quiet grace,
Caught within a dream,
In time's brief embrace.

Moments softly wane,
Like whispers on the breeze,
Joy wrapped in the rain,
Brings forth our heart's ease.

As night gives way to day,
We cherish every gleam,
In life's sweet ballet,
We dance through the dream.

Glimmers of Delight

Morning light arrives,
With sparks of vibrant hue,
In each heart, it thrives,
Awakens dreams anew.

Chasing butterflies,
Through fields where laughter swells,
Beneath the bright skies,
Where every moment tells.

A fleeting glance we share,
Encapsulated bliss,
In this world, so rare,
It's in the simple kiss.

With every laugh and sigh,
We gather treasures bright,
In the soft goodbye,
We hold the glimmers light.

Fables in the Fog

In the shroud of misty night,
Whispers dance in pale moonlight.
Tales of creatures, old and wise,
Fade like shadows, then arise.

Listen close to what they say,
Secrets kept, then drift away.
Nature speaks in hushed refrain,
Fables lost, yet found again.

Through the fog, a path unfolds,
Magic stories, time beholds.
Each footstep echoes, soft and slow,
In the realm where legends grow.

In the night, we find our place,
Every heartbeat, every trace.
Fables linger, softly bound,
In the fog, they wait around.

The Lightness of Being

Weightless thoughts on gentle breeze,
Floating high among the trees.
In the laughter, joy's sweet song,
We discover where we belong.

Moments dance like petals twirl,
In the beauty of this world.
Every glance, a spark ignites,
Within the heart, a blaze of lights.

Through the laughter, through the tears,
We embrace our hopes and fears.
Lightness comes when we let go,
Of heavy chains and doubts we know.

In each heartbeat, in each sigh,
Find the grace as time drifts by.
Being whole, not lost or bound,
In the lightness, love is found.

Drifts of Imagination

In a world where dreams take flight,
Thoughts like clouds adorn the night.
Imagination, vast and free,
Crafts the tales of what could be.

Wander far beyond the stars,
Where the moonlight softly spars.
Colors burst in mind's design,
Every whim a brilliant sign.

Through the pages, stories flow,
In the silence, imaginations grow.
Embark on quests through lands unknown,
In drifts of dreams, we find our own.

With each stroke of thought, we soar,
Opening wide imagination's door.
Dance with visions, wild and bright,
In the calm embrace of night.

Subtle Signs

In the quiet, whispers speak,
Gentle nudges, soft and meek.
Nature's rhythm, pulse divine,
Guide us close to subtle signs.

A rustling leaf, a fleeting glance,
In the stillness, we find chance.
Hearts aligned with cosmic thread,
Messages in silence spread.

Follow paths where shadows lead,
In the darkness, take the heed.
Signs may dance in light or shade,
In the tapestry we've made.

Open eyes and open hearts,
Find the magic in the parts.
In each moment, truth entwines,
Life reveals its subtle signs.

Echoes of Inspiration

Whispers dance on evening air,
Thoughts weave dreams with gentle care.
Through the silence, voices call,
Echoes rise, and shadows fall.

Hope ignites a vibrant flame,
Fueling hearts, igniting names.
In every heart, a wish resides,
In every soul, the courage hides.

Nature's palette paints the day,
Sunset's glow, in bright display.
Moments shared and laughter spread,
Inspiration's fabric led.

Through valleys deep and mountains high,
Visions soar, they learn to fly.
In every echo, life persists,
In every heartbeat, joy exists.

Mirage of Possibilities

In the desert, dreams take flight,
Mirrored visions; day and night.
Sands shift softly, time unspun,
Endless options, ever run.

Golden dunes beneath the sun,
Fleeting shadows—this racc begun.
Each step forward, hopes ignite,
Fading dreams yet full of light.

Whispers beckon from afar,
Guiding souls like a distant star.
Amid the haze, the heart finds its way,
Chasing visions, come what may.

Oh, the paths we choose to tread,
In our minds, vast worlds are spread.
A mirage leads, a fickle friend,
To possibilities without an end.

Luminous Fantasies

Stars align in twilight's grace,
Capturing light in a warm embrace.
Dreams ascend with every beam,
Awakening a world of gleam.

Colors swirl in midnight's dance,
Illusions cast in belated chance.
Vibrant tales in shadows play,
Luminous threads guide the way.

In the stillness, visions glow,
Stories told in whispers low.
Magic twirls on unseen wings,
Scripted on the heart, it sings.

Chasing whispers of what could be,
In luminous fantasies, we are free.
With every spark, our spirits rise,
In the cosmos, vast and wise.

Chasing Stardust

With every leap, we touch the sky,
Chasing stardust as it flies.
Dreams cascade like comets bright,
Filling hearts with cosmic light.

Galaxies swirl in endless night,
Each journey swathed in pure delight.
In the chase, we find our truths,
In every moment, we renew our youth.

Stars remind us of our place,
In the vastness, we embrace.
Wishes scattered like seeds of light,
Chasing stardust, hearts take flight.

So let us roam, let spirits soar,
Chasing wonders, forevermore.
In every gleam, a story told,
In chasing stardust, we are bold.

Hints of the Mystical

In shadows deep, the whispers reign,
Secrets dance, like soft, sweet rain.
Veiled in night, a glimmer shows,
A world awakened, where magic flows.

Stars align, in cosmic grace,
Echoes stir, through time and space.
Mystic realms, where shadows play,
Guiding dreams, they light the way.

Starlit Musings

Beneath the sky, where starlight spills,
Thoughts emerge like gentle thrills.
In the quiet, wishes weave,
A tapestry of hopes to leave.

Whispers soft, of night's embrace,
Time unfolds at its own pace.
In this dance of light and dark,
Hearts ignite, a sparkling spark.

Flickering Pathways

Footsteps trace on paths unseen,
Flickering light, where dreams have been.
Each turn reveals a story worn,
A journey filled with hope reborn.

Guided by the fireflies' glow,
Mysteries lie where wishes flow.
Through tangled woods, we wander far,
Chasing echoes, beneath each star.

Veils of Delight

Threads of laughter, spun in air,
Weaving joy, beyond despair.
Veils of delight, a soft caress,
In this moment, we are blessed.

Colors blend in evening's hue,
A canvas bright with love so true.
As shadows dance, we find our song,
In the heart where we belong.

Threads of Imagination

Weaving dreams in twilight's glow,
Stitching thoughts both high and low.
A tapestry of hopes untold,
With colors daring, bright, and bold.

Whispers linger in the air,
A canvas painted with great care.
With every thread, a story spun,
In the quiet, minds will run.

Through the fabric, visions dance,
In this world, we take a chance.
Entwined in creativity's thread,
Where every notion finds its bed.

In the silence, ideas bloom,
Lighting pathways through the gloom.
Threads of gold and silver shine,
In the heart, they intertwine.

Flickers of Joy

In the morning, sunlight breaks,
Sparkling rays on tranquil lakes.
Nature's laughter fills the air,
With every glimpse, a treasure rare.

Children's giggles, pure delight,
Chasing shadows, hearts so light.
Moments fleeting, yet so bright,
Flickers of joy, a sheer delight.

A smile shared, a friend nearby,
In simple gestures, spirits fly.
Collecting joys like precious stones,
In laughter, love, we find our homes.

Even in the darkest night,
Hope emerges, soft and slight.
Flickers of joy, forever glow,
Guiding hearts where dreams can flow.

A Dance of Light

Moonlight waltzes on the sea,
Gentle whispers, wild and free.
Stars align in rhythmic grace,
In the night, we find our place.

Shadows sway with soft embrace,
In a dreamlike, mystic space.
Every flicker, every beam,
Leads us deeper in a dream.

Nature's pulse, a soft delight,
Ignites the soul with purest light.
In this dance, we lose the fight,
Finding freedom, taking flight.

Each step taken, hearts align,
In this moment, we resign.
A tapestry of night unfolds,
A dance of light, as life beholds.

Ethereal Reveries

In twilight's calm, spirits soar,
Ethereal whispers at the door.
Visions floated on the breeze,
Inviting thoughts like rustling leaves.

Dreams and wishes intertwine,
In the stillness, stars align.
Moments captured, fleeting grace,
In reveries, we find our place.

Each sigh carries tales untold,
Of ancient lands and futures bold.
In the silence, secrets lie,
Like echoes of a gentle sigh.

Woven softly in the night,
One escapes into the light.
Ethereal dreams, we drift away,
In this realm where shadows play.

Tranquil Sojourns

In the hush of dusk's embrace,
Soft whispers dance on the air,
With every step, a gentle pace,
Nature's heartbeat, calm and rare.

Ripples brush the quiet stream,
Reflections of a waning sun,
Where thoughts drift like a fleeting dream,
In moments shared, we are as one.

Beneath the boughs of ancient trees,
The world slows down, begins to breathe,
Each breeze a sigh, each rustle frees,
Worries fade like autumn leaves.

Together we find solace here,
Among the blooms of fragrant peace,
Hearts whisper soft, our voices clear,
In tranquil sojourns, we release.

Patterns of the Night

Stars weave tales in the starry skies,
A tapestry of dreams unfolds,
The moonlight shines, a silver guise,
Illuminating truths once told.

Whispers linger in the cool night air,
Each shadow dances, a hidden game,
In the silence, secrets laid bare,
As constellations call my name.

The wind carries scents of time forgotten,
While owls speak in hushed delight,
Branches sway, the world feels rotten,
Yet beauty glows in patterns bright.

Lost in reverie, I gently tread,
Through midnight paths of endless song,
Each heartbeat echoes, softly spread,
In patterns of the night, we belong.

Veils of Time

Beneath the sky, where shadows blend,
Time unfurls its mystic thread,
Moments whispered, beginnings end,
In every sigh, the past is fed.

The clock ticks softly, yet we pause,
To seek the echoes of our days,
In gentle streams, we find the cause,
Of laughter shared and endless ways.

Veils of time shroud dreams once bright,
Each wrinkle tells a tale so dear,
In faded hues of black and white,
We capture joy, we conquer fear.

With every breath, new tales arise,
Threads of fate entwine and weave,
In the tapestry of our skies,
We learn to love, we learn to grieve.

The Path of Illumination

On winding roads that twist and turn,
The light ahead begins to gleam,
With every step, our hearts will yearn,
For truths that guide us, like a dream.

The morning breaks with colors bright,
Each hue revealing shades of grace,
In this journey, we find our light,
Illumination in every place.

Through shadows cast and tempests bold,
We rise again with spirits high,
For in the dark, new stories told,
Awaken hope beneath the sky.

Together, hand in hand, we stride,
With courage bright as flames that burn,
On the path of love, we shall abide,
In every heart, our souls return.

Tumbles of Inspiration

Thoughts cascade like rolling stones,
Chasing dreams where hope is sown.
In every tumble, lessons learned,
A fire inside forever burned.

Embrace the falls, the twists, the turns,
For in the darkness, passion yearns.
Each stumble shapes the journey's core,
Creating paths that lead to more.

Whispers of wonder fill the air,
In moments where we truly care.
Hearts open wide, like flowers bloom,
Bringing light to every room.

So leap and roll, let spirits soar,
In these tumbles, we'll find the core.
With every fall, we rise anew,
Transforming dreams into the true.

Hazy Horizons

A gentle haze drapes the dawn,
Where shadows linger, dreams are drawn.
Soft whispers tease the waking light,
As hope unfurls, dispelling night.

Beyond the mist, the world awaits,
With open arms and golden gates.
Each breath a promise, fresh and bright,
Guiding hearts into the light.

Colors blend in a painter's sky,
As echoes of the past drift by.
In the distance, adventure calls,
Through hazy horizons, a journey sprawl.

With every step, the vision clears,
Strengthened by laughter, softened by tears.
So chase the dawn, embrace the view,
For life's horizon beckons you.

Gossamer Threads

Delicate strands of silver light,
Woven gently through the night.
Each thread tells a story spun,
Of dreams that linger, never done.

In whispered winds, their secrets soar,
Binding hearts, forevermore.
A tapestry of hopes and fears,
Glimmers softly, through the years.

With gentle hands, create your weft,
Of love and laughter, joy bereft.
For every bond that you embrace,
Will find a home, a sacred space.

So gather threads, unite, and weave,
In this dance, we shall believe.
For in the fabric of our lives,
Gossamer threads are where love thrives.

The Language of Light

In every dawn, a story starts,
A gentle hush that warms our hearts.
In beams of gold, the truth takes flight,
Speaking softly in the light.

Colors dance on nature's stage,
Painting wisdom through each page.
From shadows deep, to radiant beams,
The language of light, woven dreams.

With every flicker, a secret shared,
In sunlight's touch, we feel prepared.
To walk the paths where hope ignites,
Embracing joy, dispelling nights.

So let us listen, feel, and see,
In the glow of light, we find the key.
For in this language pure and bright,
Lies the essence of our flight.

Whispers of Enchantment

In the twilight's gentle glow,
Magic dances, soft and slow.
Whispers float on the night air,
Secrets hidden everywhere.

Stars will twinkle, dreams take flight,
Underneath the silver light.
Promises in the shadows weave,
Leaving hearts that dare believe.

Echoes of a world unseen,
Where the mundane meets the dream.
With each breath, the magic swells,
In the silence, wonder dwells.

Embrace the night, let it seep,
Into the corners of your sleep.
For in the stillness, life's romance,
Awaits in every whispered chance.

Fleeting Hues

Morning breaks with colors bright,
Painting dreams in rosy light.
Golden rays on dewdrops gleam,
Nature hums a vibrant theme.

Crimson skies at dusk unfold,
Tales of warmth that must be told.
With each sunset, shades will fade,
Fleeting moments, memories made.

In the shadows, colors play,
Chasing light, they drift away.
Hold them close, but understand,
Every hue slips through your hand.

With each season's turn and sway,
Life's palette shifts, come what may.
Capture joy in every view,
For beauty lies in fleeting hues.

Shadows of Curiosity

In the corners, shadows creep,
Secrets buried, hidden deep.
Questions dance within the dark,
Seeking answers, igniting spark.

Footsteps echo in the night,
A flicker of a distant light.
Whispers call from realms unknown,
Challenging the brave alone.

What lies beyond the veil of fear?
Mysteries close, yet far and near.
Each enigma feeds the soul,
A quest that makes the spirit whole.

So wander into the unknown,
Embrace the path that's yet unshone.
For in the shadows, truth will gleam,
Awakening the wildest dream.

Secrets on the Breeze

A gentle breeze whispers low,
Tales of places we don't know.
Secrets carried far and wide,
On the wind, old stories ride.

Rustling leaves, a soft refrain,
Songs of joy, heartache, and pain.
Listen closely, hearts will find,
Wisdom whispered, intertwined.

As clouds drift across the sky,
Echoes of a distant sigh.
Nature speaks in subtle ways,
Guiding us through winding days.

So take a moment, feel the air,
Embrace the secrets waiting there.
For life's essence, pure and free,
Is found within that gentle breeze.

The Magic Between Moments

In whispers soft, the night unfolds,
A tapestry of dreams retold.
Each heartbeat counts, a fleeting spark,
Connecting worlds within the dark.

A glance exchanged, a treasure found,
In silence, echoes dance around.
The pulse of time, a gentle flow,
In every pause, new wonders grow.

A fleeting smile, a breath of air,
Moments weave through threads of care.
In tiny glimmers, hope ignites,
The magic lives in simple sights.

As shadows stretch to meet the dawn,
In every day, a dream is drawn.
From darkness blooms the light we see,
Embrace the magic, let it be.

Serene Sparks

In gentle waves, the silence hums,
From whispers deep, a stillness comes.
Each spark of light, a fleeting chance,
In nature's arms, our spirits dance.

The soft embrace of twilight's glow,
As stars align, the heartbeats flow.
In tranquil skies, the secrets blend,
Awakening dreams, like rivers bend.

A breeze that sighs, the trees respond,
In quietude, our souls are fond.
Each moment blooms, a fleeting grace,
Our hearts ignite in this safe space.

Serene the world, where we belong,
In every sigh, there's whispered song.
Together here, we find our way,
In harmony, forever stay.

Traces of the Unseen

Beneath the surface, secrets hide,
In layers deep, where dreams abide.
Each shadow casts a silent trace,
Of stories lost in time and space.

The echoes linger on the breeze,
In rustling leaves, in whispered trees.
Each footstep tells a tale unknown,
Of paths unworn, of seeds once sown.

A glance, a sign, the heart perceives,
In every moment, magic weaves.
The unseen threads bind us as one,
In the quiet dusk, where lives are spun.

Beyond the veil of what we see,
Awaits the dance of mystery.
In the stillness, life unfolds,
The traces speak of tales untold.

Flights of Fancy

With wings of dreams, we soar the skies,
In vibrant hues, where hope defies.
Each thought a feather, light and free,
A journey wide, for hearts to see.

Through clouds of whimsy, laughter flows,
In playful winds, our spirit glows.
The magic swirls, imagination's flight,
In endless realms, we chase the light.

A castle built on dreams so bright,
Adventures dance in day and night.
Beneath the stars, our stories blend,
In flights of fancy that never end.

So let us wander where dreams abound,
In laughter's echo, joy is found.
With every heartbeat, let's embrace,
The boundless skies in our shared space.

Shimmers of Serenity

In the still of night, stars twinkle bright,
Soft whispers of peace, taking flight.
Moonlight dances on tranquil seas,
Embracing the world, like a gentle breeze.

Dreams drift slowly on clouds of gray,
Carried away by the dawn of day.
In the warmth of sunlight's glow,
Serenity blooms, allowing joy to flow.

Through the rustling leaves, a calm refrain,
Nature's embrace, washing away pain.
Moments of silence, pure and profound,
In this stillness, true beauty is found.

Let the shimmers guide without fear,
Leading us home to what we hold dear.
In the heart's sanctuary, we ignite,
The magic of peace in the soft moonlight.

Magical Murmurs

Whispers in twilight, secrets untold,
A story unfolds, as night turns bold.
Gentle breezes carry a tune,
Under the watchful gaze of the moon.

Voices of shadows play hide and seek,
In the heart of the night, nature speaks.
Murmurs of magic, soft as a sigh,
Echoing softly as time passes by.

Stars share their wisdom, ancient and wise,
In the quiet moments, under the skies.
Each note a treasure, full of delight,
Carried on beams of shimmering light.

In this realm where stillness thrives,
The essence of wonder truly arrives.
Embrace the whispers, let them be heard,
In the language of beauty, in every word.

Echoing Laughter

In the fields where children roam,
Laughter rings out, a joyful home.
Chasing the sun, hearts light and free,
Wrapped in the warmth of camaraderie.

Every giggle dances on the breeze,
Bringing a smile with effortless ease.
Echoes of joy, a melody sweet,
Filling the air where friends meet.

Moments captured in the blink of an eye,
Sparks of happiness, soaring high.
Through the shadows, their spirits shine,
In a world where laughter intertwines.

Let the echoes remind us to play,
In the spirit of youth, come what may.
For in the laughter, we find our way,
A chorus of joy that will never fray.

Glints of the Infinite

In the vast cosmos, we seek to find,
Glints of the infinite, intertwined.
Stars like jewels, scattered in grace,
Whispering secrets of time and space.

Galaxies swirl in a dance divine,
A symphony played on the cosmic line.
Wonders await with each daring gaze,
Guiding lost hearts through the cosmic maze.

Every twinkle a promise, a dream to unfold,
Countless stories in stardust told.
Among the constellations, our spirits soar,
Searching for meanings, forevermore.

In the quiet night, let us revel and roam,
Chasing glints of the infinite, calling us home.
For within the universe, vast and grand,
Lies a journey waiting, a wondrous strand.

Glimmers of Enchantment

In twilight's grasp, the stars ignite,
Soft whispers dance in silver light.
A world awash in shimmering hues,
Where magic blooms in morning dew.

Beneath the arch of ancient trees,
The gentle rustle in the breeze.
With every step, new tales unfold,
A tapestry of dreams retold.

With every shadow, every laugh,
The heart awakens to its path.
A glimmer here, a spark of grace,
We chase the light; we find our place.

In gardens where the wild things grow,
The secrets of the night bestow.
With eye agleam, we search anew,
In glimmers bright, our spirits flew.

Whispers of the Unknown

In silence deep, the shadows sigh,
Veiled mysteries call from nearby.
With every breath, the secrets swell,
In whispered tones, they weave their spell.

The moon bequeaths her silver kiss,
A tender touch, an echo's bliss.
The stars align, a hidden fate,
Unraveling threads that weave our state.

Through veils of mist, the pathways wend,
Whispers of journeys yet to end.
Eager hearts, they lead the way,
Into the night, where dreams shall play.

We follow where the calling leads,
With open minds and daring deeds.
Each step we take, a door we find,
Unlocking realms of the divine.

Threads of Magic

In the loom of night, the stars conspire,
Threads of magic, they lift us higher.
With every stitch, a story spun,
In patterns bright, our hearts now run.

Woven wisps of dreams take flight,
Entwined with hopes that grace the night.
In whispered spells, we catch our breath,
Embracing life, we dance with death.

The tapestry of fate unfolds,
With secrets deep and tales of old.
Each shimmer bright, a fleeting glance,
In threads of magic, we find our chance.

With gentle hands, we weave our truth,
In patterns rich, preserving youth.
Bound by the warmth of dreams so bold,
Our spirits rise, our hearts consoled.

Flickers of Dreams

In the dawn's light, the visions gleam,
Flickers of dreams dance in the stream.
On every wave, a promise lies,
A symphony beneath the skies.

With whispered hopes, we walk along,
The melody of life, our song.
In each heartbeat, a wish takes form,
In flickers bright, the soul is warm.

Through shifting sands and fleeting time,
We seek the peaks where hopes do climb.
In starlit nights, we chase the gleam,
To find our way within the dream.

With open hearts, we rise and soar,
In flickers of dreams, we seek for more.
The horizon calls, we greet the day,
With every dawn, we find our way.

Radiance in Riddles

In shadows where secrets reside,
A flicker of light starts to glide,
Chasing the whispers of doubt,
Illuminating what it's about.

Each riddle wrapped tight in disguise,
Reflects the truth through curious eyes,
Unfolding the layers of time,
As we venture through thoughts, we climb.

Answers glimmer like stars in the dark,
Guiding us gently, igniting a spark,
With every question, the world expands,
Radiance blooming from unseen lands.

So let us dance in the twilight's embrace,
Embrace the unknown, as we chase,
The mysteries hiding in plain sight,
In the riddle's heart lies the purest light.

Kaleidoscope Fantasies

Colors swirling in vivid delight,
Twisting and turning, a beautiful sight,
In dreams where the impossible glows,
Every heartbeat, a story that flows.

Fragments of laughter, shards of the past,
Reflected in patterns, forever they'll last,
Infinite visions, a canvas so bright,
Captured in shadows, embracing the light.

We wander through tunnels of vibrant arrays,
Each step revealing a new world that plays,
In the kaleidoscope's flicker and gleam,
Where fantasy dances within every dream.

United through shades of joy and despair,
In this mosaic of life, we share,
Together we weave through this wondrous trance,
Lost in the beauty, forever we dance.

Gentle Touches of the Muse

Whispers float on a soft summer breeze,
Caressing the heart, putting minds at ease,
The muse arrives with a tender sigh,
Awakening dreams that long to fly.

Like petals that fall in a sunlit glade,
Inspiration blooms; no moment must fade,
Each thought ignites a creative spark,
Illuminating pathways once hidden and dark.

With gentle touches, she crafts and she molds,
A story of life that endlessly unfolds,
In every quiet moment, a chance to explore,
Her presence lingers, forever adored.

Through ink on the page, we dance and we sway,
Guided by visions that won't drift away,
Together we sing, in harmony fused,
Finding our voice through the muse we've used.

Lullabies of the Night

Stars blanket the sky, a soft lullaby,
Whispers of dreams that gently float by,
In the arms of the night, we find our peace,
As the world hushes, our worries release.

Moonlight drapes softly, a silvery veil,
Guiding our thoughts on a sweet, silent trail,
With every breath, let the magic unfold,
A tapestry woven of nights to behold.

In shadows that dance, the dreams softly call,
Cradling wishes, no fear of a fall,
With lullabies humming, we travel afar,
Beneath the watchful gaze of a distant star.

So close your eyes and drift into the night,
The gentle embrace holds you just right,
For in this realm, every heart takes flight,
Wrapped in the warmth of sweet lullabies' light.

Hints of the Extraordinary

In shadows cast by moonlit trees,
A whisper stirs the gentle breeze.
Hints of magic linger near,
In every flicker, every cheer.

Stars align with secret grace,
A fleeting glimpse of a hidden place.
Beyond the veil, the wonders play,
Inviting hearts to drift away.

The world transforms with every sigh,
Beneath the vast, enchanting sky.
Moments catch like dew on leaves,
In the quiet, the spirit believes.

Awake the dreams that softly bloom,
In corners bright, dispelling gloom.
Expect the extraordinary today,
Embrace the magic in every way.

Elusive Encounters

In the stillness, shadows dance,
Elusive whispers seek their chance.
Glimmers fade before the dawn,
Leaving minds to ponder on.

Each gaze a brush with fate's design,
A fleeting moment, a secret sign.
Echoes linger, soft yet bold,
Stories waiting to be told.

Paths cross briefly, like a sigh,
In crowded streets, souls wonder why.
A heartbeat shared, the world expands,
In silent wonders, time withstands.

Capture fleeting, tender dreams,
In the spaces where magic gleams.
The dance of life, both lost and found,
In elusive encounters that astound.

Fantasies Adrift

Sailing on a sea of stars,
Dreams take flight, escaping bars.
Fantasies drift like clouds on high,
Painting stories in the sky.

Each wave a chance for hearts to soar,
With every swell, we long for more.
Caught in currents of delight,
We chase the visions through the night.

Whispers of adventure call us near,
With every heartbeat, we persevere.
Waves of wonder, tides of grace,
We lose ourselves in time and space.

Castles made of stardust rise,
In shimmering light, our spirits fly.
Embrace the night, dreamers adrift,
In the gentle embrace of the universe's gift.

The Soft Footsteps of Dreams

In the quiet of the night,
Dreams tiptoe in, gentle light.
Soft footsteps echo in the mind,
A tender touch, so rare to find.

They weave through thoughts like a breeze,
In whispers, they aim to please.
Calm and sweet, they softly tread,
Fueling hopes where shadows fled.

Each sigh a promise, softly made,
In realms where time and space do fade.
Carried on the wings of night,
The soft footsteps bring delight.

Awakening the heart's embrace,
In dreams we find our truest place.
Let them wander, let them play,
For in their warmth, we drift away.

Sketches of the Infinite

In the quiet whisper of the night,
Stars unveil their ancient light.
Softly they sketch the endless lies,
Infinite dreams in cosmic skies.

Time drips slowly, a silver thread,
Woven tales of what lies ahead.
Every moment, a brushstroke bold,
Painting stories untold, behold.

In the canvas of silent space,
Galaxies twirl with elegant grace.
Each flicker, a secret, a glimpse,
Of the boundless where wonder simps.

As echoes of laughter resound,
On distant shores, where hope is found.
We are but sketches in this vast,
Infinite dance, forever cast.

Drifting Through Possibility

On a breeze that knows no end,
We wander where the sky will bend.
Floating softly, like petals fall,
Through paths of dreams, we heed the call.

Each moment, a river we tread,
Where futures whispered softly spread.
With open hearts, we chase the light,
In realms where shadows take to flight.

Horizons stretch with colors bright,
Illuminating our shared plight.
Adventures beckon, wild and free,
In the dance of sweet possibility.

Hand in hand, we roam this place,
In the tapestry of boundless space.
Every step a new story spun,
In the journey that's just begun.

Clouds of Intrigue

Gray mists gather, thick and high,
Veiling truths that linger nigh.
Whispers swirl in the shrouded air,
Secrets borne on winds of care.

Beneath the veil, shadows play,
Echoes of what words won't say.
In drifting puffs, our minds take flight,
Chasing riddles into the night.

Every cloud, a tale untold,
Mysteries that gently unfold.
With every glance, intrigue grows,
In the silence where passion flows.

Let us wander where skies entwine,
In the dance where fate aligns.
Together we'll chase those fleeting shapes,
Through clouds of intrigue, our hearts escape.

Light in the Gloom

When darkness drapes the weary earth,
A flicker sparks, ignites rebirth.
In shadows deep, hope starts to bloom,
Embracing light within the gloom.

Amidst the night, a candle glows,
In quiet corners, warmth bestows.
Each flickering flame whispers near,
Tales that banish doubt and fear.

In the depths where silence reigns,
The heart beats on, through joys and pains.
Light dances softly, breaking free,
Guiding the way for you and me.

We rise and shine, like stars above,
In every shadow, there's a love.
Together we'll seek out the beam,
Finding solace in the dream.

Unseen Pathways

In shadows where whispers dwell,
Footsteps trace untold stories,
Twilight dances with the stars,
Guiding hearts to secret glories.

Beneath the veil of silent night,
Dreams intertwine like tangled vines,
Each turn reveals a hidden light,
Where hope and wonder gently shines.

Lanes of silence, paths of grace,
Each breath a dance with the unseen,
Lost in the quiet, find our place,
Emerging from what might have been.

Through the mist, our journey flows,
Bound by trust, we walk as one,
In unseen pathways, truth yet grows,
Awakening when day is done.

Affinities with the Arcane

In shadows cast by ancient lore,
Whispers of magic fill the air,
Veils of time, a mystic door,
Unlocking secrets, rare and fair.

Stars align in patterns strange,
Invoking spells both bright and dark,
In realms where reason's bound to change,
The heart's call leaves an indelible mark.

Winds of wisdom, softly sweep,
Guided by forces none can see,
In the quiet, knowledge seeps,
Binding souls in unity.

Through tangled roots of twilight's hue,
We dance with shadows, hearts aflame,
Each revelation, pure and true,
In affinities with the arcane.

Efflorescence of the Spirit

From fertile grounds, the spirit blooms,
Colors burst forth, joy takes flight,
In every petal, life resumes,
Whispers of love in purest light.

Sunlight kisses the morning dew,
Nurturing seeds of hope's ascent,
In vibrant hues, our dreams break through,
Renewed and loved, we find content.

In gardens wild, the heart expands,
Nature's touch, both soft and grand,
Embracing all with gentle hands,
Awakening to life's demand.

With each breath, the spirit grows,
A dance of petals in the breeze,
In efflorescence, beauty shows,
A tapestry of endless ease.

Melodies of the Mind's Eye

In the stillness, echoes play,
Harmonies of thought unwind,
Each note a memory, a ray,
Painting visions of the mind.

Waves of sound, a gentle stream,
Flowing through the landscape's grace,
Every whisper forms a dream,
In this vast, creative space.

Caught in rhythm, lost in time,
Symphonies of heart and soul,
Melodies begin to climb,
Revealing parts that make us whole.

In the cadence, life unfolds,
Notes that swirl, alive and free,
The melodies of stories told,
Resound in the mind's bright sea.

Shadows of Curiosity

In the corners of the mind, they stir,
Whispers of truths yet undiscovered.
Glimmers of light in the dark, they blur,
Inviting the seeker to venture further.

With each question, the shadows dance,
Guiding the heart through paths unknown.
In the silence, there's a secret romance,
As layers of thought are gently sown.

A flicker here, a glint of thought,
Unraveling worlds hidden away.
In the chase, a solace is sought,
Where wonders reside, and fears decay.

Through the maze of the mind we roam,
Following paths that ever twist.
In shadows we weave a makeshift home,
Embracing the thrill of the unexplored mist.

Echoes of the Unseen

In the quiet, whispers float around,
Echoes of dreams that never fade.
Voices softly woven into sound,
Carrying stories that time has made.

Forgotten tales on the wind do glide,
Cloaked in silence yet deeply heard.
From realms of shadows, they provide,
A glimpse of faith, a whispered word.

In the depths of night, they call to me,
Persistent as stars, silent yet bright.
In their presence, I long to be,
Drifting through the unending night.

Each echo weaves a tapestry grand,
Of moments lost, yet ever near.
In the unseen, we take our stand,
Embracing the wisdom wrapped in fear.

Breezes of Imagination

Gentle winds of thought arrive,
Carrying the scent of dreams anew.
In every breath, we come alive,
Painting the skies in shades of blue.

Whispers of stories yet untold,
Swirling softly through each open door.
In our hearts, the seeds unfold,
Beneath the surface, magic's core.

With every gust, we take our flight,
Soaring high on wings of thought.
Chasing visions that spark the night,
In the realm of dreams, all is sought.

Breezes that linger, soft and kind,
Wrap us gently in endless grace.
In their embrace, we seek and find,
A world transformed, a boundless space.

Prelude to the Extraordinary

In the hush before the dawn of night,
A promise drifts upon the breeze.
Hints of wonder, fragile and light,
Gathering strength as the heart sees.

With each moment, the stage is set,
For tales that linger just beyond sight.
In dreaming eyes, we dare to get,
Lost in the dance of shadows and light.

A glimmer here, a spark of time,
Where ordinary meets the divine.
In the silence, a whispered rhyme,
Hints at magic in every line.

So let us pause to feel the sway,
Of moments weaving through the now.
In prelude to the grand display,
We find the courage to take a bow.

Fragments of the Surreal

In a dreamscape where shadows play,
Whispers dance in a murky sway.
Faces form through vapor's breath,
In colors that flirt with life and death.

Brittle clocks melt on the ground,
As words float gently without sound.
Mirrors crack in strange designs,
Reflecting thoughts like tangled vines.

Birds with anchors soar the skies,
Chasing echoes of silent cries.
A tapestry of thoughts unwound,
In the realm where lost is found.

Surreal dreams weave tales of grace,
In the corners of a forgotten place.
Mystery runs like a hidden stream,
Through the fragments of each dream.

Sunbeams in Twilight

When daylight bows to the evening star,
Golden rays flicker from afar.
A canvas painted with hues of gold,
Stories of warmth in shadows told.

Whispers of dusk in a gentle breeze,
Kissing the leaves of ancient trees.
Softly the twilight weaves its thread,
In the twilight where dreams are bred.

Glimmers of hope in the fading light,
Flicker and dance, a wondrous sight.
As stars emerge in the sapphire sky,
Sunbeams linger, and then say goodbye.

Reflecting the last of the sun's sweet glow,
While secrets and wishes begin to flow.
In this moment, all is still,
Sunbeams and twilight our hearts fulfill.

Rainbows of the Mind

In a prism bending light so bright,
Thoughts collide in colors of delight.
Every hue a whisper, a tale to tell,
In the realm where dreams and visions dwell.

Crimson hopes and azure fears,
Swirling memories through the years.
Golden laughter and emerald tears,
Paint the canvas of shifting spheres.

A splash of violet in the gray,
Brightens the shadows that linger and sway.
Rainbows weave paths of vibrant grace,
Uniting moments in time and space.

The mind a garden where colors bloom,
Filling the heart, dispelling the gloom.
In every thought, a spectrum shines,
Crafting a world where the spirit aligns.

Portraits of Serendipity

In quiet corners where fate conspires,
Moments unfold like flickering fires.
Chance encounters in a fleeting glance,
Life paints portraits of the unexpected dance.

The laughter shared over cups of tea,
An open heart, a wild spirit set free.
Wonders bloom in the simplest things,
As fortune sings with invisible wings.

Paths intertwine in a cosmic play,
Guided by serendipity's sway.
A gentle nudge, a call to embrace,
The beauty of life in its random grace.

Each serendipitous twist and turn,
Teaches the heart what it yearns to learn.
In the tapestry woven with love and art,
Portraits of dreams unfold in the heart.

Sighs of the Sky

Clouds drift softly by,
Whispers of the night.
Stars blink in rhythm,
Glimmers of quiet light.

Moonlight bathes the earth,
In silvered embrace.
Dreams float on the breeze,
A peaceful, gentle space.

Raindrops tap a tune,
Nature's tender call.
Each sigh tells a story,
Of winter, spring, and fall.

In the canvas above,
Colors blend and sway.
The sky, a vast wonder,
Paints magic every day.

Glows of Serenity

Morning brings the light,
Soft hues fill the air.
Nature wakes in grace,
A moment, pure and rare.

Trees sway gently now,
In harmony and peace.
Birds chirp a sweet tune,
A symphony's release.

Rivers softly flow,
Mirroring the sky.
In this blissful world,
Time gently drifts by.

As shadows stretch and fade,
The sun begins to set.
In golden warmth, we find,
Serenity beget.

Breaths of Magic

Evening casts a spell,
In twilight's soft embrace.
The stars begin to dance,
In the cosmos' wide space.

Whispers of the night,
Carry tales untold.
Magic fills the air,
In the dark, a world of gold.

Moonbeams knit the dreams,
Of lovers, old and new.
Each breath a promise made,
In the night's shimmering blue.

As this magic weaves,
A tapestry of light,
We surrender to the night,
In wonder and delight.

Reverberations of Elegance

Leaves whisper secrets soft,
In the cool evening shade.
Every flutter speaks love,
In nature's grand parade.

The breeze carries notes,
Of elegance and grace.
In every corner found,
A beauty we embrace.

Mountains stand so proud,
Guardians of the land.
Echoes of the past,
In their silent command.

As dusk paints the sky,
With hues both bold and bright,
We find our souls entwined,
In the elegance of night.

Milton Keynes UK
Ingram Content Group UK Ltd.
UKHW022117251124
451529UK00012B/566

9 789916 905395